Bring Love

Written by Brittany Gibbs

Illustrated by Jana Borja

D1501111

Dedication

To my daughters, Joey & Jordan, may you always show compassion and have the courage to do the right thing.

About the Book

This book is written from the perspective of my six year old daughter who has a different skin color than most of her friends and recognizes that her appearance is unique and should be embraced. The hope of publishing this book is that it can be a useful resource for families to help in teaching their children about diversity and race.

My family may look different than yours, but different is pretty great.

We don't have matching skin colors or hair textures either, ranging from very curly to stick straight.

We may not look alike,
but looks are
not important.

What matters is that we
love each other,
with every single ounce.

It's so special to be unique,
that's what makes the
world have flare.

Some people may laugh
and tease me,
but I own my curly hair!

Most kids in my school don't look the same as me, which some people don't understand.

I try to encourage them to learn about diversity and offer them a helping hand.

It doesn't matter how you look, it's what's on the inside that counts.

I am taught to treat everyone the same and show compassion in great amounts.

At times, the world can be hard for kids trying to fit in and be cool.

Although most people are kind and caring, there are people who can be cruel.

It is important to stand up for what's right, remaining quiet does no good.

You see, sometimes people may feel out of place, confused or misunderstood.

I am blessed to be brave enough to speak out and do the right thing.

That's what makes the world a better place, it's all about what you bring.

Bring love, bring understanding, bring compassion, bring kindness, bring light!

About the Writer

Brittany Gibbs lives in New Hampshire with her husband, two daughters and two Boston Terriers. She wanted to provide a book for families to help create dialogue about race and diversity. Brittany's hope in writing her first book is that it inspires parents to have these important conversations with their children, using her book as a guide. After all, the world can always use a little bit more love, kindness and compassion.

Photographs taken by SummerGrace Photography

Made in United States
North Haven, CT
04 October 2022

25018910R00024